Your Child's Early Development Made Simple:

An Essential Guide and Keepsake Book

Arielle Rigaud-Riveira, MD

Nathalie McNeil, PT, DPT, CEIM

DEDICATION

This book is dedicated to ALL families because kids don't come with a manual but many times parents wish they did!

CONTENTS

ACKNOWLEDGMENTS

We wish to express our sincere gratitude to our families for all of their support and patience throughout the process of writing this book. Additionally and most importantly, we want to thank those families who helped create our vision of this guide. It was through their requests to have a manual to help them better understand their little ones, that we became motivated to create one.

INTRODUCTION

Deciding to have a family and the offspring that follow is one of the most fulfilling experiences one can go through. With this newly created life, comes an abundance of joy, love, fear, and responsibility. As parents, we want to provide the very best and help our child in every possible way. We want to give them every advantage and assist them with every disadvantage so that they can be healthy, successful, and positive members of society. Much like building a house, children need a solid foundation from which to grow big, strong, and independent. If this is not provided or established, the difficulties can be plentiful which can impact the child, their family, their community, and society. It is therefore, of the utmost importance that as parents we are equipped with the best knowledge about how to help guide our children so that a solid foundation is created. Part of that guidance may include the need to have a basic understanding of development so that it can be monitored. Development is formally defined as the growth of an individual throughout their lifespan. Early development is that growth which occurs during the early years of a person's life. Our guide will focus on the changes that occur in the first three years of life and in five specific areas: cognition, language, self-help, social emotional, perceptual fine motor, and gross motor.

The current Centers for Disease Control and Prevention (CDC) statistics reveal that 17% of children are challenged with some form of developmental or behavioral disability and less than 50% of those children are being identified prior to starting school.[1] This is a startling statistic given that under The Individuals with Disabilities Education Act (IDEA), early identification and intervention is mandatory.[1] Additionally, a 2012 CDC statistic, estimates that 1 in 88 children have been identified with an autism spectrum disorder (ASD).[2] Research shows that early identification of delays and early intervention can improve a child's development.[3,4] Early intervention services are for children up to three years of age and are designed to address delays in any of the following areas: physical, cognitive, communication, social/emotional, and adaptive. As two health care professionals immersed in early intervention, our main goal is to educate and to increase the sensitivity of monitoring the developmental health of children. We essentially want to bridge the gap between caregivers and the medical community to help decrease the amount of children that fall behind unnoticed. As two parents and two healthcare professionals, we are well positioned to help bridge this gap.

In order to reach our goal, we chose to model our guide after the age ranges and developmental subsections of the Developmental Programming for Infants and Young Children, Early Intervention Developmental Profile (DPIYC) by Sally Rogers, Carol M. Donovan, Diane B D'Eugenio, Sara L. Brown, Eleanor Whiteside Lynch, Martha S. Moersch, and D. Sue Schafer.[5] The DPIYC is one of the products of the Early Intervention Project for Handicapped Infants and Young Children created in the 1970's.[5] It was originally created to describe the developmental status of a child 0-36 months in 6 areas of development.[5] Even though the test has not been standardized, the assignment of items to specific age ranges were based on standardizations or research from other instruments.[5] The DPIYC continues to be a commonly used tool in the therapeutic community to describe developmental status or level of delayed children. It is frequently used because it is simple to administer, provides more detailed information about reflexive and cognitive development, and provides developmental sequences in multiple areas. Although there are other developmental screener tools available for parents, the DPIYC provides short age intervals making monitoring of milestones more frequent which is the goal of our guide. The checklists in this guide contain some major milestones from the DPIYC. It is not the actual DPIYC test, which is more comprehensive and requires professional training to administer. The checklists in this guide are purely to monitor your child's development and not to diagnose a delay or a condition. Remember that if your child develops skills faster or slower than indicated in the checklists, it does not mean that there is a delay and your child may be developing just fine. As always, if you have any questions or concerns contact your Pediatrician or trusted health care provider.

The path down parenthood is one of those unique journeys, which evokes every possible emotion known to mankind. Take time to enjoy your child and savor every minute and every accomplishment as time truly goes by too fast. The following chapters are intended to provide you with the knowledge to help guide you with the developmental milestones of your little one. Together we will embark on the journey of growth and development and share with you the very special moments of those first smiles, words, and steps that bring so much joy.

* As you begin to read this guide, please keep the following in mind. Always supervise your baby especially when he/she is on their tummy and follow the current American Academy of Pediatrics guidelines of placing your baby on their back to sleep. Make sure that you always use infant approved toys to stimulate your baby taking special precaution that he/she does not play with anything he/she can choke on. This serves as a guide to monitoring your child's development and not to diagnose a delay. It is not intended to serve as a replacement but rather a supplement, to your Pediatrician's management and advice on your child's developmental health.*

CHAPTER 1

THE FOUNDATION

Becoming a parent is one of the most challenging and rewarding experiences one can have. Once your new little bundle of joy arrives, the decisions and responsibilities are overwhelming. Parents do the best that they can with the information they have available. They quickly realize that these little extensions of themselves do not come with a manual. Parents become focused on changing diapers, feeding, sleeping, schedules, and let us not forget the rest of their regular routine that existed prior to their baby's arrival. With all that parents have to focus on, it is easy to imagine how developmental milestones may not be the center of attention. Our hope is that this guide will serve as an easy way of monitoring development as well as being a useful tool to communicate with your Pediatrician your baby's developmental health.

As per the CDC 17% of children have developmental delays of some sort and less than 50% are being detected prior to school age.[1] As you can see there is a large gap in the detection or evaluation system of developmental milestones in young children. If we want to help our children succeed, we have to as a society collectively increase our sensitivity and awareness about the developmental health of all children. We have to get more involved in early detection and prevention so that the delays can be addressed early to maximize progress and minimize future challenges. We are here to guide you through the daunting process of raising a healthy, well rounded, and independent child. This guide has been designed to guide you in monitoring your child's development in real time, within small age ranges from zero up to three years of age in all areas of development.

Developmental milestones are age specific achievements that the majority of children accomplish by a certain age range. Every developing child is unique and will achieve these milestones at different times within the associated age range. The goal is to help your child in the critical early stages establish a strong foundation in all areas of development, which she/he can then build upon for future successes. The most challenging part as a parent is recognizing when a key milestone has been missed and what to do about it. We will help you recognize when your baby is not on track so that you can intervene early and help your baby when it is most important. If you were blessed with the early arrival of a baby, you are probably wondering if you have to do anything different to monitor development. Full term babies are those babies born between 37 and 40 weeks gestation. A baby's due date is calculated to be 40 weeks gestation. Premature babies are those born under 37 weeks. When looking at their development it is common for practitioners to consider both their actual age (chronological age), which is their age from time of birth and their corrected age. Corrected age takes into consideration the number of weeks a baby was born prematurely from 40 weeks and then subtracts from the actual age. As a guide, there are roughly 4 weeks per month therefore, if a child is born 4 weeks early their adjusted age will take that into account. To further explain this point if you have a baby who is 8 weeks old (2 months) and was born at 36 weeks gestation, he was born 4 weeks early. Therefore if his actual age is 2 months old, his adjusted age is 1 month old (40 weeks - 36 weeks = 4 weeks correction needed, so corrected age is 8 weeks - 4 weeks = 4 weeks or 1 month). It is common practice to monitor a premature child by their corrected age and the expectation is that by 2 years of age they have caught up to their actual age. Some practitioners however like to monitor both chronological and corrected age. This allows for earlier detection of areas you as a parent can focus on at home.

We have provided developmental checklists to be used as a tool to communicate with your Pediatrician according to our sharing schedule also enclosed. We encourage you to copy them and post them on your fridge so that you can check off the milestones your child has accomplished and by when. Additionally we have included a chapter of developmental red flags, which covers critical milestones and behaviors that may signal the need for further medical or developmental evaluation. Our goal is to bridge the gap between the medical community and caregivers in order to minimize the amount of children who slip through the cracks developmentally. Ultimately, we want to help inform caregivers of all kinds and increase the overall sensitivity surrounding developmental issues. **It is important to take these checklists with you to your baby's well visits according to our sharing schedule so that your Pediatrician can also follow how your baby is doing developmentally and decide when intervention is necessary and appropriate. Missing a milestone or achieving a milestone late does not mean that your child is delayed. The key is to monitor and share with your Pediatrician so that a decision can be made as to when further evaluation is necessary.** The key to developmental health is identifying delays early, so that the appropriate intervention can be provided. The first step to monitoring your child's developmental health is understanding development and the different developmental areas, which the next chapter explains.

CHAPTER 2

AREAS OF DEVELOPMENT

As with everything in the human body, nothing is isolated, it is all interconnected and interrelated. The same is true for human development. Key milestones are not isolated to just one area of development. Achieving a milestone in one-area sets up the foundation for others to follow in multiple areas of development. There are six key areas of development that this guide will focus on and that your baby will be making gains in. Those areas of development are as follows:

Cognition

Language

Self-help/adaptive

Social/ emotional

Perceptual/ fine motor

Gross motor

Cognition: Skills in this area of development are gained by your child's ability to process information from his environment as well as his ability to acquire knowledge through reasoning and perception. Piaget, a famous Swiss psychologist who was the mastermind behind the theory of cognitive development, established a framework from which children learn.[6] Following his framework, children develop through two different stages of cognitive development. From birth to 24 months children are considered to be in the sensorimotor period, which means that learning during this stage is based primarily on the senses or sensory system and movement.[6] Your child through hearing, smelling, touching, and tasting will learn about their immediate environment. As they move and experiment with their environment, they develop an understanding of *cause and effect*, imitation, communication, and *object permanence*. These skills allow them to move and act upon their environment in a purposeful manner to learn from it and get their needs met. From two to six years children enter the preoperational period where they learn to differentiate words and images from the actual objects and events.[6] It is during this time of development that children gain the skills of matching, sorting, memory, and the concept of numbers. Achieving key milestones in this domain enables children to problem solve, reason, imitate, recognize, communicate, and understand concepts.

Language: Language can be broken down into two subsections, which include receptive and expressive language. *Receptive language* starts out with basic hearing then progresses to the appropriate understanding of the spoken sounds and words. It allows for recognition of where sound is coming from, orientation to one's name, association of words with objects/people, and following commands or directions. *Expressive language* includes the child's ability to vocalize sound, cry, imitate sounds, use variations of intonations, and use words and gestures to communicate. During the first year of life, children quickly move from the stage of crying to selectively making sounds, which include imitating sounds and some single words. By the second year a baby learns to attach more meaning to what he is saying and begins combining words to communicate his needs. By the third year, most babies have roughly 900 – 1000 words and can readily combine them to pose and answer questions and communicate more elaborately their needs.

Self-help/Adaptive: Skills in this area is what allows a child to become self sufficient with what is termed activities of daily living (ADL): feeding, dressing, hygiene, and toileting. In the beginning, children are completely dependent upon their caregivers to meet their basic needs. They will be breastfed or bottle fed, dressed, bathed, and diaper changed. As they get older and progress, they will start taking food from a spoon, will learn to take shoes off, and will let their caregivers know when they need their diaper changed. By three, they will be able to feed themselves, can put on and take off their clothes, can help during hygiene activities (bathing, brushing teeth, washing hands, combing hair), and should be on their way to mastering toilet training. This area is crucial to master as it contains the basic functions of a human, which enable one to become self-sufficient and independent.

Social/ Emotional: Humans are social creatures by nature. We seek relationships and interactions with others. A strong foundation in this area is crucial to their childhood development. As children grow and develop, they learn that they are a separate being from their caregivers whom they are dependent upon. Slowly they experiment with independence by attempting to do things all by themselves, saying no to adults, and exploring new places. They learn about their caregivers by exploring their faces as they are being cared for. They begin smiling at games of peek-a-boo, begin to place names to faces, they learn their name and age, recognize family members, know whether they are a boy or a girl, and learn to share and take turns in play. This foundation sets them up for a lifelong journey of interacting with fellow citizens so that they can become productive members of society.

Perceptual/Fine motor skills: These skills include your child's ability to use his senses to process the information in his environment and respond appropriately. These skills also include his ability to use the smaller or fine muscles in his hands to manipulate objects and toys. Children first master the use of their vision to look, process, and learn about their environment, which includes focusing on objects or people, following moving objects, and responding to different light intensities. These achievements create the foundation for the next step, which includes reaching out touching and manipulating those objects with his fingers and hands. As they mature they learn to build towers, make objects with modeling clay, color, cut, write, create representations of what they see, and manipulate buttons and zippers for dressing.

Gross Motor: This area of development includes all major movements in the body, which eventually allows children to be independent within their environment. Through normal neuromuscular development, primitive reflexes disappear and children begin learning about their body, how to control their bodies, how to balance, how to use both sides of their body together to coordinate movements, and explore different ways of moving. As with other areas of development, babies are first completely dependent and can not even hold their head up. As they grow and get stronger, they advance to rolling, sitting, crawling, and walking to name a few. These key milestones enable children to explore their environment independently so that they can learn from it and socially interact with others.

Now that we have a better understanding of the different areas of development, let us explore the different age ranges and see what specifically happens at these times. Please remember that each area of development does not fit into a neat little box. The following sections include developmental milestones checklists, developmental red flags, common questions to ask your Pediatrician, and important health information to have handy. Use this guide to document your baby's achievements and share it with your Pediatrician as a tool for monitoring their developmental health. Additionally, it can also double up as a keepsake book celebrating all your baby's firsts.

CHAPTER 3

DEVELOPMENTAL MILESTONES CHECKLIST

This chapter provides parents and caregivers with checklists to complete accompanied by a sharing schedule so that parents know at what well baby visit to give a copy of a particular checklist to their Doctor. The goal is to document when a milestone has been achieved i.e. sitting at 6 months. We encourage parents and caregivers to make copies of the checklists so that they can be shared with the Pediatrician during our recommended times as per the included sharing chart. This will help your Pediatrician follow how your baby is doing developmentally and decide when and if intervention is necessary and appropriate. Our hope is that this will help parents, caregivers, and Pediatricians keep track of your baby's developmental health in an easy to follow format and aide in facilitating developmental dialogue. Missing a milestone or achieving a milestone late does not mean that your child is delayed. The key is to monitor and share with your Pediatrician so that a decision can be made as to when further evaluation and intervention is necessary if at all. We do not want parents to become nervous when a milestone has not been achieved. We encourage parents to share the checklists with their Pediatricians during our recommended sharing schedule, which coincides with certain well baby visits. At that appointment, your Pediatrician will decide whether they want to take a wait and see approach, which is common or take further action.

When to Give a Copy of the Checklist to my Doctor and Which One

Well Baby Visits Birth – 12 Months

Checklists	2 week	2 month	4 mths	6 mths	9 mths	12 mths	Comments
Birth-2 mths	No list	X	No list *				* Keep in mind that some 2-month milestones may not be achieved because of timing of visit. If not all filled in, bring in during 4 month visit as well *
3-5 mths				X			
6-8 mths					X		
9-11 mths						X	

X= At what well baby visit to give specific checklist to Pediatrician

Well Baby Visits 15 – 36 Months

Checklists	15 mths	18 mths	24 mths	36 mths	Comments
12-15 mths	X				Keep in mind that some 15-month milestones may not be achieved because of the timing of visit. If not all filled in, bring in during 18 month visit as well
16-19 mths		X			Keep in mind that some 18-19 month milestones may not be achieved because of the timing of visit. If not all filled in, bring in during 24 month visit as well
20-23 mths			X		
24-27 mths				X	If by 30 mths, not all filled in, consider following up with Pediatrician
28-31 mths				X	If by 34 mths, not all filled in, consider following up with Pediatrician
32-35 mths				X	

X= At what well baby visit to give specific checklist to Pediatrician

Your Child's Early Development Made Simple

Birth to 2 Months Milestones

next to individual milestones, write the age when it was achieved. If it has not been achieved, leave it blank

Cognition	Age	Language	Age	Self-Help	Age
Brings hands to mouth	2m	Cries when hungry or to be held		Nurses or drinks from a bottle	
Brings hands to mouth		Makes different sounds- cries, coos, gurgles		Coordinates well sucking, breathing, swallowing while feeding	
Repeats random movements such as kicking legs alternately		Startles at sound by 2 weeks			
		Responds to sounds by moving arms, legs, eyes			

Social Emotional	Age	Perceptual Fine Motor	Age	Gross Motor	Age
Begins to calm down to caregiver's voice or face		Looks at face while being fed, held, & cuddled		Requires full head support when carried	
Soothes with thumb sucking or pacifier		Visually follows moving object, person, light that is close		At first will still be in fetal position with arms and legs bent	
Makes brief periods of eye contact		Maintains hands in loosely fisted position		Momentarily holds head up while on tummy	
Begins to smile to touch or when talked to				Begins turning head side to side on tummy	
				By the second month will relax arms and legs a bit and straighten out partially arms and legs	
				Emerging head control	

Notes/ observations/ favorite moments:

Dr. Rigaud & Dr. McNeil

3 to 5 Months Milestones

next to individual milestones, write the age when it was achieved. If it has not been achieved, leave it blank

Cognition	Age	Language	Age	Self-Help	Age
Brings hands to mouth	2 m	Has different cries (hunger, tired, soiled)		Continues to breast or bottle feed	
Looks at toys held		Vocalizes when talked to (reciprocal)		Brings hands to breast or bottle	
Shakes rattle to make noise when placed in hand		Turns head towards a sound source		May start baby foods with spoon at end of this stage if baby is holding head up well (based on MD advice)	
Brings toys & hands to mouth to explore		Makes sounds of happiness squealing or other high pitched noises (gurgles & coos)			
Tracks moving objects					

Social Emotional	Age	Perceptual Fine Motor	Age	Gross Motor	Age
Makes eye contact with caregivers (3 mths)		Maintains hands open		Begins rolling from tummy to back (by end of stage)	
Watches adult walk across the room		Plays with hands bringing them together		Pulls self to sitting when hands are held with no head lag	
Smiles at familiar people		Begins reaching for objects by batting at them		Props up on forearms when on tummy	
Smiles or laughs during physical play		Holds objects with entire hand using mostly palm		Begins to explore grabbing feet and toes	
Soothed by parent's voice when crying				Bears weight on feet when held	
				Good head control when trunk is supported	

Notes/ observations/ favorite moments:

Your Child's Early Development Made Simple

6 to 8 Months Milestones

next to individual milestones, write the age in months when it was achieved. If it has not been achieved, leave it blank

Cognition	Age	Language	Age	Self-Help	Age
Brings hands to mouth	2 m	Continues to vocalize sounds including consonants (b, m, p)		Begins to take food from a spoon	
Pulls a blanket off of his face		Localizes where a sound is coming from		Closes lips on spoon to get food	
Looks to the floor when something falls		Plays with variation of voice (volume and pitch)		Typically eats stage 1 and 2 baby foods	
		Begins to babble "ba-ba" or "ma-ma"		Picks up spoon	
		Reciprocal vocalizations continue			

Social Emotional	Age	Perceptual Fine Motor	Age	Gross Motor	Age
Smiles at social games like peek-a-boo		Picks up smaller objects like cheerios using multiple fingers – raking grasp		Reaches for toys while playing on tummy	
Shows preference for being with people and for certain objects/toys		Picks up a cube/block using fingers		Experiments with getting on hands and knees	
Explores features of an adult face (eyes, ears, nose)		Transfers toys from one hand to another		Masters rolling from tummy to back and back to tummy	
Reaches for self in the mirror				Sits independently	
Attachment to caregiver is established and stranger anxiety may begin later in this stage				Combat crawls (on tummy)	
				Moves from sitting to hands and knees and may start rocking	
				Supports most of weight through legs while in supported standing	

Notes/ observations/ favorite moments:

Dr. Rigaud & Dr. McNeil

9 to 11 Months Milestones

next to individual milestones, write the age when it was achieved. If it has not been achieved, leave it blank

Cognition	Age	Language	Age	Self-Help	Age
Brings hands to mouth	2 m	Imitates sounds (consonant-vowel combination i.e. ba)		Holds bottle to feed himself	
Finds objects that are out of sight or hidden (object permanence)		Imitates non-speech sounds such as coughing, clicking, etc.		Feeds himself bite size pieces of food i.e. cheerios *"finger feeding"*	
Begins to imitate simple facial gestures		Inhibits activity in response to "no"		Eats soft crackers by chewing on them with gums not just sucking	
Explores smaller parts of toys i.e. poking eyes of dolls		Looks at familiar objects or persons when named		Begins to eat some mashed table food	
Bangs toys together		Responds to name when called			

Social Emotional	Age	Perceptual Fine Motor	Age	Gross Motor	Age
Participates in simple social games		Picks up small objects like cheerios with thumb and pointer finger *"fine pincer grasp"* by end of this stage		Crawls well on hands and knees (creeping)	
Offers a toy or object to caregiver		Plays with blocks (bangs them together & drops them into a container)		Has good balance reactions in sitting	
Does things for attention i.e. squeal, dance, act silly, etc.		Pokes things using just the pointer finger		Pulls up to a standing position holding on to object or person	
Leaves physical contact with caregiver momentarily- separation anxiety				Walks while holding on to furniture "cruising"	
Responds to joint attention – follows a point to look at what parent wants to share with them				Stands with out support for a few seconds	

Notes/ observations/ favorite moments:

Your Child's Early Development Made Simple

12 to 15 Months Milestones

next to individual milestones, write the age when it was achieved. If it has not been achieved, leave it blank

Cognition	Age	Language	Age	Self-Help	Age
Brings hands to mouth	2 m	Uses 1 word meaningfully by 12 mths		Tries to brush own hair	
Stacks blocks to build a small tower (2 blocks)		Follow a simple direction *"one step command"* i.e. come here with gesture at 12 mths & w/out gesture at 15 mths		Uses sippy cup or straw cup for drinking	
Imitates an action on a doll such as kissing or rocking it		Shows a body part when asked (15 mths)		Drinks from open cup when held by adult	
Finds toys correctly when hidden (under one of 2 cups)		Uses 3-5 words at 15 months		Tries to use spoon to feed himself with a lot of spills (15 mths)	
		Uses gestures to communicate (points to desired object at 12 mths)		Cooperates and helps with dressing and diaper changes	
		Imitates words inexactly		Takes off shoes & socks	

Social Emotional	Age	Perceptual Fine Motor	Age	Gross Motor	Age
Asks for things by pointing		Starts scribbling with a crayon after shown how to (15 mths)		Walks by himself (12-13 mths)	
Shows awareness and interest in other young children		Puts small item (cheerio/raisin) into a small container (15 mths)		Moves from sitting to standing without holding on to anything	
Initiates social games with adults		Turns pages of a thicker book		Squats to pick up objects	
Leaves contact with familiar person repeatedly to play		Takes lids off of small boxes		Pushes and pulls toys	
Shows empathy (15 mths)		Builds a 2 cube/block tower		Walks backwards by the end of this age range i.e. pulling a toy	
Shares something by pointing to it and looking to make sure caregiver is seeing it				Crawls up stairs	
				Throws a ball (end of this range)	

Notes/ observations/ favorite moments:

Dr. Rigaud & Dr. McNeil

16 to 19 Months Milestones

next to individual milestones, write the age when it was achieved. If it has not been achieved, leave it blank

Cognition	Age	Language	Age	Self-Help	Age
Brings hands to mouth	2 m	Can understand and carry out 2 familiar directions i.e. "come here" and "sit down"		Drinks from an open cup without help with some spilling	
Identifies a few familiar pictures in a book 1 picture by 18 mths		Uses a few single words to get needs met 10-25 words at 18 mths		Feeds himself with a spoon with spilling	
Begins to play with simple puzzles		Identifies multiple body parts (3) by 18 mths		Discriminates what is edible and not	
Problem solves to reach objects out of reach i.e uses a stick		Points to a named object in a book by 18 months		Tries to wash hands but needs help	
		Names one object when asked		Cooperates with tooth brushing	

Social Emotional	Age	Perceptual Fine Motor	Age	Gross Motor	Age
Shows interest in children and may begin approaching them		Scribbles with a crayon		Begins to walk up stairs with help	
Plays apart from familiar person ~5 minutes		Tries to imitates simple crayon strokes by end of age range i.e. a line		Climbs onto furniture i.e. sofa, chair	
		Builds tower with more cubes (3-5)		Can balance on one foot with help	
		Begins to show a right or left handed preference		Beginning to run may look stiff	
				Throws ball with more force	
				Crawls downstairs (by end or range)	

Notes/ observations/ favorite moments:

18

Your Child's Early Development Made Simple

20 to 23 Months Milestones

next to individual milestones, write the age when it was achieved. If it has not been achieved, leave it blank

Cognition	Age	Language	Age	Self-Help	Age
Brings hands to mouth	2 m	Imitates new sounds and words and imitates simple 2 word phrases by 23 mths		Can drink from a straw cup.	
Can do simple puzzles i.e. square, circle, triangle		Identifies familiar objects by naming them (at least 3)		Takes off some articles of clothing	
Imitates body motions i.e. stomp feet, clap hands, etc.		Has > 25 words		Attempts to put shoes on may be on wrong foot	
Begins to match objects by items i.e. blocks with blocks, spoons with spoons, etc.					

Social Emotional	Age	Perceptual Fine Motor	Age	Gross Motor	Age
Interested in playing close to other children or along side of them, but may still be timid		Imitates simple crayon strokes lines and circular strokes		Jumps with feet together in place	
Displays independence, does not want help		Holds crayon with fingers		Goes down stairs with hand held	
Begins to put toys away when asked		Continues playing with blocks building larger towers (6 cubes)			
Imitates household chores such as sweeping					

Notes / observations / favorite moments:

19

24 to 27 Months Milestones

next to individual milestones, write the age when it was achieved. If it has not been achieved, leave it blank

Cognition	Age	Language	Age	Self-Help	Age
Brings hands to mouth	2 m	Puts 2 words together to make simple phrases consistently (24 mths)		Eats with a spoon and with few spills	
Points to 5-10 pictures when asked		Sometimes will refer to self by using his name		Begins using a fork to pinch food	
Begins matching objects by color (2 colors or more)		Vocabulary of 50 words by 2 years old		Begins toilet training (24 mths) and expresses the need to go, by 27 mths has few accidents	
		Identifies 4 or more objects when named		Drinks from a straw (24 mths)	
				Takes off clothes (24 mths)	

Social Emotional	Age	Perceptual Fine Motor	Age	Gross Motor	Age
Begins "*parallel play*" playing along side other children		Can copy more accurately a vertical line and a horizontal line (24 mths)		Goes up/down stairs alone	
Likes to make choices now, what to wear, what to play with, etc.		Plays with jars screwing and unscrewing lids		Stands on a balance beam or narrow surface and takes a step	
Engages in familiar activities like pretending to be on the phone, cleaning, etc. by 24 mths		Lines up two or more blocks as if putting together a block train		Jumps with feet together	
				Kicks a ball	
				Throws ball overhand	

Notes/ observations/ favorite moments:

Your Child's Early Development Made Simple

28 to 31 Months Milestones

next to individual milestones, write the age when it was achieved. If it has not been achieved, leave it blank

Cognition	Age	Language	Age	Self-Help	Age
Brings hands to mouth	2 m	Responds to questions about location i.e. Where is the cat?		Washes and dries hands with help	
Identifies object by use (cup, spoon, ball) i.e. What do you drink with?		Able to understand some prepositions (under, behind, in, etc.)		Spoon feeds well with minimal spilling	
Matches objects by color (4 or more colors)		Uses simple pronouns i.e. me, you, etc		Puts on simple clothes without assistance	
Understands the concept of one				Uses fork well	
Social Emotional	Age	Perceptual Fine Motor	Age	Gross Motor	Age
Plays with other children		Builds a tower with 8 bocks/cubes		Can walk on tip toes	
Identifies himself in the mirror		Makes a train with blocks (3 cubes for train and a smokestack)		Takes a few steps on a balance beam	
				Throws ball underhand up in the air	

Notes/ observations/ favorite moments:

21

Dr. Rigaud & Dr. McNeil

32 to 35 Months Milestones

next to individual milestones, write the age when it was achieved. If it has not been achieved, leave it blank

Cognition	Age	Language	Age	Self-Help	Age
Brings hands to mouth	2 m	States his complete name		Masters toilet training	
Matches shapes (4 or more)		Asks a lot of questions where, what, etc.		Gets drink from simple water source independently	
Repeats 2 numbers stated		Follows 2 step commands well (sit down and take off your shoes)		Gets dressed independently	
Sorts by shape and color		Uses prepositions to answer where questions (under, in, behind, etc)		Undoes large buttons, snaps, shoelaces, zippers	
		Begins to count		Washes and dries hands independently	

Social Emotional	Age	Perceptual Fine Motor	Age	Gross Motor	Age
Interactive play with other children		Copies a circle by end of this age range		Goes up stairs alternating feet while holding onto a railing	
Shares toy with adult help		Cuts with child safe scissors		Stands on one foot and balances by end of this range ~ 3 sec	
Separates from caregiver in unfamiliar environment for ~5 min.		Strings beads on a rope (5 or more)		Starts to ride a tricycle by end of this age range (35 mths)	
Has an active imagination and may have some fears by end of this stage				Runs well	
Identifies own sex					

Notes/ observations/ favorite moments:

22

CHAPTER 4

DEVELOMENTAL RED FLAGS

Although each child is an individual and develops at their own rate, failure to reach certain milestones or presence of specific behaviors may signal the need for further medical or developmental evaluation. Eventhough the below is categorized by age, the presence of the listed items below persisting beyond the associated age range may signal the need for further evaluation. If you notice any of the following red flags in your child, discuss them with your pediatrician and/or qualified health professional.

By 4 months

- Doesn't seem to respond to loud sounds
- Doesn't follow moving objects with her eyes
- Doesn't attempt to bat towards objects
- Doesn't hold objects placed in their hand
- Cannot support her head, it falls forward/backward when not supported at the neck
- Does not make eye contact with caregiver
- Does not begin making cooing type sounds

By 8 months

- Seems very stiff, with tight muscles
- Seems very floppy, like a rag doll
- Head still flops back when pulled up to a sitting position
- Doesn't bear some weight on legs when held in standing position

- Avoids eye contact
- Keeps hands mostly in a fisted position
- Not being able to move or open one hand or arm
- Only kicks or moves one leg
- One or both eyes frequently turns in or out
- Does not respond to sounds nearby
- Has difficulty getting objects to mouth
- Does not smile by six months
- Does not begin babbling
- Shows no interest in games of peekaboo
- Not pushing up on straight arms while on tummy
- Does not like being held

By 13 months

- Does not crawl on belly by 10 months
- Does not crawl on hands and knees by 12 months
- Does not get into sitting position and sit independently by 10 months
- Does not pull to stand by 12 months of age
- Drags one side of body while crawling (for over one month)
- Cannot bear full weight in a supported standing position
- Does not respond to name
- Does not attempt to use simple words to call parents ("mama" or "dada")
- Does not use gestures, such as waving, pointing, or shaking head
- Does not point to objects or pictures
- Does not imitate banging objects together like blocks after demonstration
- Does not hold her bottle by herself or needs to lay down in order to hold the bottle
- Does not clap her hands together by 12 months after demonstration
- Does not pick up small objects using two fingers
- Consistent coughing or choking while eating or drinking

By 18 months

- Cannot stand alone without support by 14 months of age
- Does not finger feed by 15 months
- Cannot walk by eighteen months

- Does not speak at least ten to fifteen words by eighteen months
- Does not initiate joint attention which is pointing to something to share with a parent and looking at parent to make sure they are looking at that object by 15 months
- Not able to eat a variety of textured foods (only eats purees)
- Does not help with dressing activities (pushing arms through sleeves, pushing legs through pants, etc.)

By 2 years

- Does not use two-word phrases by age two
- Does not imitate familiar actions or words by age two
- Does not follow simple one step instructions by age two (kiss mommy, come here)
- "Walks" their hands up their legs to get into a standing position from the floor
- Only walking on their toes, not the soles of their feet
- Frequent falling, tripping, or loss of balance
- Always holds objects close to face to see them
- Does not engage in pretend play by 28 months
- Overly sensitive to familiar loud noises i.e. vacuum cleaner, blender, blow dryer, etc. (covers ears, screams, runs away)
- Shows no interest in other children, prefers to play alone
- In perpetual movement with a short attention span i.e. will not attend to simple story or simple game with caregiver

CHAPTER 5

COMMON QUESTIONS FOR WELL BABY VISITS

Once your baby is born, you and your family are going to be adapting to the many changes of having a baby in the house. Apart from the feeding, burping, diapering, and nurturing you will be doing, well baby visits will be commonplace in your hectic schedule. In order to minimize stress and additional thinking, we have compiled a list of questions that you can have ready to ask your Pediatrician for every well baby visit up to 3 years of age.

2 week visit

- Can you review the general care of a newborn: feeding, sleeping, stooling, bathing?
- Can you review breast feeding and formula options and general guidelines on how to feed my child?
- What are some symptoms my child might display that would be considered an emergency and require me to call you right away?
- How is my baby's weight gain? Has my baby regained his birth weight?

2 month visit

- Is my baby gaining the right amount of weight?

- Can you briefly review the vaccine schedule for my child?

- When is tummy time good for my child and when is it dangerous?

- When should I be concerned about vomiting with my child?

4 month visit

- Can you discuss ways for me to start a routine for my child?

- Can you discuss how and when to start baby foods and spoon-feeding?

- Can my babies stooling pattern start changing now?

- Can you discuss teething and what to expect?

- Do I need to supplement with any vitamins or minerals?

6 month visit

- Can you give me recommendations for safety proofing my house for the baby?

- How do I manage colds and fever in an older infant?

- What are some age appropriate toys I can buy for my baby now?

8 or 9 month visit

- When do I start introducing finger foods?

- Can you tell me more about walkers?

- How do I manage diarrhea and vomiting with my child?

- Do I need to screen my child for increased lead levels and anemia?

12 month visit

- What do I need to know about ear infections?

- How do I transition my child to table foods and whole milk?

- How do I prevent my child from choking on things?

- Even though my child passed her newborn hearing screening, does she need to repeat a hearing test for any medical reason?

- If my child falls and hits their head what are the basic things I should know to do.

15 month visit

- How is my child doing with their weight and growth?

- How do I handle picky eating?

- When can I consider changing my child to a toddler bed?

18 month visit

- When do I consider toilet training my child?

- Can you discuss the benefits of a preschool or playgroups for my child?

- Can you discuss the management of fever and colds in toddlers?

- Is there anything you are concerned about with my child that would make you want to see her before the next check up at 2 years of age?

24 month visit

- How can I manage temper tantrums?

- What if my child does not want to stop taking her bottle and/or pacifier?

- If my child is still a picky eater do I need to supplement with vitamins? How is my child growing?

- What should I be doing for dental care at this point?

- Is there anything you are concerned about with my child that would make you want to see her before the next check up at 3 years of age?
- If my child falls and hits their head now, do I need to follow the same steps I would have followed when they were an infant?

36 month visit

- What safety precautions should I be taking now that my child is more independently active (bicycle helmets, falls, head trauma)?
- Do I need to consider vision or hearing screening for my child?

CHAPTER 6

INFORMATION A PARENT SHOULD HAVE AVAILABLE FOR THEIR CHILD'S PEDIATRICIAN

- **Pregnancy history of the mother:**

  Including whether prenatal care was given, results of any fetal ultrasounds, amniocentesis results (if done), chronic or acute conditions of the mother during pregnancy, and any drug or alcohol use.

- **Birth history:**

  Including gestational age of the child at birth, type of delivery, APGAR scores, complications during delivery or following birth, time spent in the hospital, whether the newborn hearing test was passed, and if the child received the Hepatitis B vaccine in the hospital. If your baby was recommended to follow up with any specialist after being discharged, have handy who and why. If your child was in the NICU always ask for a copy of the discharge summary from the hospital prior to leaving.

- **Family history:**

  This should include knowledge of both medical and developmental history. Common conditions that can be inherited include speech delays, learning disabilities, mental illnesses, genetic syndromes, epilepsy, autism spectrum disorders, dyslexia, asthma, eczema, allergies, diabetes, kidney problems, cancers, thyroid conditions, and certain conditions causing anemia such as sickle cell disease.

- **Social history:**

  This should include knowing who lives in the house with your child. Who the primary caretakers are and if this includes daycare or preschool. It would also be helpful to be able to explain what kind of routine you have set for your child. Major changes in your child's social setting should always be mentioned to the Pediatrician.

- **Other medical specialists, therapists, and evaluations:**

  If your child has seen a professional other than his Pediatrician, it is always helpful to bring a copy of their report summarizing their visit to the Pediatrician to review. You can always ask any specialist for a copy of their report following your visit with them.

- **Medication:**

  If your child is taking medication you should be able to give the Pediatrician the name and dosing of the medication. If your child is given herbal or alternative medicine it is also wise to mention this to the doctor. While they may not be familiar with all types of alternative medicines, doctors are now more aware of the more common ones and may be able to look up information for you regarding them.

- **Developmental history:**

  Knowing the timing of the major milestones is also helpful. For example, when your child sat, crawled, walked, said his first word, etc. **Fill out the charts in this guide and give your Pediatrician a copy according to the sharing schedule in this guide (chapter III).**

- **Medical History:**

  If your child has a chronic or reoccurring condition this is important to mention. Examples can be asthma, eczema, heart murmur, kidney problems, etc.

- **Illnesses:**

  If your child is sick with fever it is wise to take the temperature and be able to report how high and how long the fever has been there. Also if your child is with vomiting and diarrhea, you should be able to describe how often in a day he is going to the bathroom, how often you noticed him urinating, and keep track of the liquids they are able to drink and keep down without throwing up. Knowing the quality of the stool may be helpful as well. For example if there is mucous or blood present in the stool and whether it is watery or just loose. If your child has been with cold symptoms including congestion and/or cough, you should have an idea of how long they have had those symptoms and if there was anything that made the cough better or worse.

Special Moments

Picture

Special Moments

Special Moments

Picture

Picture

Special Moments

Special Moments

_____
_____
_____
_____
_____
_____
_____
_____
_____
_____
_____
_____

Picture

Picture

Special Moments

Picture

REFERENCES

[1] Centers for Disease Control and Prevention Online, "Developmental Screenings," http://www.cdc.gov/ncbddd/actearly/pdf/parents_pdfs/developmentalscreening.pdf (accessed 03 April 2012).

[2] Centers for Disease Control and Prevention Online, "Act Early," http://www.cdc.gov/ncbddd/actearly/ (accessed 03 April 2012).

[3] Handleman, J.S., Harris, S., eds. Preschool Education Programs for Children with Autism (2nd ed). Austin, TX: Pro-Ed. 2000.

[4] National Research Council. Educating Children with Autism. Washington, DC: National Academy Press, 2001.

[5] D. Sue Schafer et al., Developmental Programming for Infants and Young Children, vol. 1-3, (Michigan: University of Michigan, 1977).

[6] Piaget, J. (1983). Piaget's theory. In P. Mussen (ed). Handbook of Child Psychology. 4th edition. Vol. 1. New York: Wiley.

ABOUT THE AUTHORS

Arielle Rigaud-Riveira, M.D.

Dr. Arielle Rigaud is a mother of two children currently living in South Florida with her family. She grew up mostly in South Florida but also has spent some time living in California. She received her Bachelors of Science degree from the University of Miami with a major in Psychobiology. She went on to achieve her medical degree at the University of Miami Miller School of Medicine. Her residency was completed at Jackson Memorial Hospital where she specialized in Pediatrics. She practiced as a Pediatrician in a private practice setting for five years and then began practicing Developmental Pediatrics. She always had a special interest in Early Childhood Development and it is through her practice that she realized the need to further educate parents on their children's developmental health.

Nathalie McNeil, PT, DPT, CEIM

Dr. Nathalie McNeil is a mother of two children who currently lives in South Florida with her family. She grew up in the United States Virgin Islands. She received her Bachelors of Science degree from Florida International University with a major in Health Education, her Masters degree in Physical Therapy from Nova Southeastern University, and after practicing for some years went on to earn a Doctorate in Physical Therapy. Additionally, she is a Certified Educator of Infant Massage and has a passionate interest in educating parents about early childhood development. She has been working with children since 1999 and has been involved with early intervention evaluation and treatment since the beginning of her career.